THE POEMS OF EMILY DICKINSON

THE   MS OF M Y   KIN

W0010607

THE MS OF MY KIN

JANET HOLMES

SHEARSMAN BOOKS
EXETER

First published in the United Kingdom in 2009 by
Shearsman Books
58 Velwell Road
Exeter EX4 4LD

http://www.shearsman.com/

ISBN 978-1-84861-035-4

Many thanks to the editors of the following journals for publish-
ing some of the poems herein, occasionally in different form: *1913,
Cannibal, Coconut, Cultural Society, Cutbank, Gutcult, Jumps, Mel-
ancholia's Tremulous Dreadlocks, MiPoesias, Notre Dame Review,* and
Practice: New Literature + Art.

Gratitude also to the following institutions: Boise State University
(for a sabbatical leave), The Foundation Ledig-Rohwolt and the
Chateau de Lavigny, The Idaho Commission on the Arts, and The
National Endowment for the Arts (US).

Cover design by Quemadura.

These poems are erased from Emily Dickinson's poems of 1861 and 1862, the first years of the United States Civil War. Each poem of mine is titled by the year in which Dickinson composed the original(s), its order in the current sequence, and (in parentheses) the Franklin numbers of the erased poems. I owe the project to the invitation of its epigraph.

If it had no pencil,
Would it try mine —

E.D., #184

AGAIN, FOR AL

at

Sunrise —   a Flag

How short it takes to make

                    Victory

                              hear them

            bustle

    fumble at   Prayer —

            coming
                          before

The   Country

Martyrs —
Their

Company —

Streaks
Opon a Planet's

Air —

then

two
come

No
No

Dawn

means   Risk —
Revelation —

Apocalypse —

Anguish

again —

Transport

        clad in

      a trick

Does'nt —   move —

       without

              me —

God gives us

      Victory —

               lips

take it —

    so economical

       little mouths

know how to starve —

Confronting
  the Adamant

Mind

          near his nest

        how late — how late —

Transporting

           the fire   burn

      the Centuries

                   men

    fumbled

Till those two troubled

         the Desert
With

a fine invention

Emergency

more distinctly seen —
                    the surge

                    reached the other side —

Come slowly

Round

Least   docile

Yield

Reeling —

                              renounce

                                          the

                                                     hunt —

          lost   World —

Give
A Memorial   —

      no
      Granite   !

      an Organ

           no word —
      breath

           what was done to me

      one cannot
      transport

      Ghosts in Cages

What sorcery

    would not

                        do,

    they

Did

        Heart!

        Heart —

                when Time is over —

    will   each separate

tell

his woe

the

long
late morn

Elephants

rose   their

gales

the eyes
shone

quiet   of death —

A Witch   yieldeth

to

my will
If anybody
care

You

cheated
grinning

night will   be
home to

a little dull
pain

welcome

I
spotted

a little thing —

    yet

          I was strong

          He was strong

Neither — was strongest —

       somebody bring the light
So

Death wont hurt —

       light —
       setting sun

awful

creatures

shook their fists —

finished that

Girl's life

Stop there!

plea —

Oh God!

Her
Heart —

I hear the

transport

— in brass and scarlet —

It is

Men
service in the place
Where

Wilderness — can be

Desert Noon —

we hide our brave

dream

to the end —

Take us   Lord —

He   — and I   remembered

                                   fire

A Slash

                            between

                           eyes

That hunted —

                          it broke

        useless as   morning's

blame

going
Home

Some
        wear   Wings —
      instead

                        the Heart

    sent

  To climb

            at your side

staggered —

Try —
Try —

dream

it's

play

the fall of

Who live there —

they know

the soul   in pain —

simple,

Like a Panther

dropped

Into
a Face
suddenly

Death
drills his Welcome in

"Found dead" —

the Setting Sun

supremer —

spangled   —

The

One!

It matters

that the oil
is gone.

One life
　　　　　　would pay —

　　　Pearl —
That

　　　cost

　　burns

The
    Bad men

           offended

    his

    Empire

    intercede

If
 —
                nothing — more

God —

the pulse *just*

quivering —
"consider"

that
Some   were moved

By   *trust* —

These
fetching Stars

puzzle us

the

Company

shift s
tone

to fear —

wrestles

Forgets

all

Cuckoo

rules   —

Britain

discerns

shining   a

Retreat —
America —

No Trace   of the Thing
That dazzled

Men, and Feats

swallowed up

like   Blood

the puppet
just now

quivered out   —

It

— concernless   —

Nods

Decades of Arrogance

Nobody

admiring

The day

gone —
now   remembrance

You are
no one

Or

very far

from me —

time for me

to walk

away
beloved Heart —

we can never learn
Change —

It cant be
    got through!

   that long town of

    "Dying"

    shall go in

  Cuffs

            see his face?

  that is not
        let

You know who

        "shares"

Dominions—

Now

        pay
                    this

    Contract

        's worth

Rearrange a
                    Brain!
Amputate
                a man!

        spirit, in thy
        unacknowledged

Constancy

None suspect

                        it's *bandaged* —
will never get away

                    see   them
                        shut the door!

Oh,   the Gentleman
In   "White Robe" —

                        forbid?

Wild

Wild

            Heart
Done with

                    singing

Late —

Over the fence

would

climb —

Captive!

ashamed of that

Dishonor

bend   low

Again —   voice   at the door

to *justify*
He never *saw*   *this*

The *other's*

Dog

Goes

First

to
The   *Vein* —

doomed
to die
unheard —

Civilization

never rebuked her

She was

the
keeper —

Pity   left her

Going to
Tell
Tell
Tell

they

You
Tell

were silenter

begged to be ended —

That day

      the Souls that
      Elected

     Subterfuge

                carved away
Behold

The World

     bears another's — name —
        if it be fair

The Man —   the Woman —

or a lesser

superior

qualified for

our new
Tactics

should have been

blamed —

should have had
the Fear

to understand

The Zeros
            learned to like

                                    power

                 That
                        smites
                 And

                                    appalls

                 suggests

                 the

Whip

Until Death touches
it

chanting "Live"!

She tied the Hoods to

every shoulder

to hide

Who

affronts

The   men

Elephant
Look further   .

others — show

Like Juggler's Figures

It   halts —

Denying   it was —

got so
            Tremendous
That Stop-sensation
And Thunder —

                  that forcing,

            to   Extremity —

Petition's
         ignorant

      Business —
         Power
Not subject to

                  the Soul

                    put away
                              as if no plight
        Had

            just turned

    Into Eternity —

                    the Peril's

        greater than
    They

    Will   it   —

A Weight

this

Heart
had not strength to hold —

Fantastic

Mystery!

Night after Night

men
vanish   !

The Doomed
With   Delight —

The Man — to die — tomorrow —

Joyful —

Joyful —

Just one
Charge

                    men
                              who prefer   the Glory
And their

        God's

                    martial

                              march

farther Parted, than

Twelve months ago —
We

the patientest

— how soon?

It's

    Everlasting

They have no

    Home

    Coming

    they're never   —

Heaven

Lift
            the Boy —

Homesick   steadfast   —
Ah —

            Escaped —

They cannot take

        Guns

As

        a Travelling Show
   who died   yesterday

      for

       souls — away —

Who is to blame?

God should

drop a life

Into

plummetless

bliss

then —

softly —

stirless —

Kill

reach

"Heaven"   —   !

The
        interdicted Land —

        Paradise —

        spurned us —

1862.9 (311–312)

off the Road

two
hand the Tools

by night
a
gag   —

None

see who's there

A Watch

sleeping —

Screams

And Echoes —

just

Pools of

Pain

How many
How many

"Hope" is the

tune without the

Bird

the chillest
strangest

sunshine

That once
Blazed

    in my   gazing — face —

            now —   it

Turns   away

that flight

Struck

Lives —

leaves the shreds behind—
Oh
Come back —

You
You

Her

So distant —

Universe,

vaster
And

Completeless

There's a certain

Heft

.

Shadows — hold
                like
            Death

                    quenching
                the Sky

                    's

                    Candle

        — for You

the Dark

might have been

the Camp —

Men
And   Women
Passed
Into

the Desert

a Day

no Soul

Was

Permitted to

look

at   the Grave

1862.13 (325–327)

lonesome for

the old Mountains

Scarlet

lip

the odd

Kennel —

Just
Solitude —

They

who overcame

"Defeat"

stood — whispering

the Flesh
        wants
    more —

                               snap

        Life   up —
   Deliberate, as
      Kingdoms

                 do

He had no

conversation —

was

appalling

Dim

the Life —

the Woman

ceded all of

Heaven,

laughter

like
the Tide's

weep

for the Sorrow, done me —
Joy

despatched abroad

the Boughs

Beyond
Beyond

Hid

Birds

        Grace   —
       Outcast   —

parted Rank —

hurt
herself,
a Ball she got —
And

happy   sudden —

smiling —
Just consummated —
this one, wears
pain
Fresh

I got my eye put out —

                                    my Heart
        split,

The Meadows —
The Mountains —
All Forests —

                finite

The Motions of
    Morning's

        news   strike me dead —

The

                                 Oddity —

       we buried

      the Jacket   he
     buttoned in the
             mornings,

The

  Tie

The Beads

                        strung

Service

                    Boots

                an Ear,

Wrecked,

And
And
And
And

so appalling

To know the worst

The Truth,

If
We

Stop

Just let

Others   wrestle

Terror's

O'ertakeless

Sweep

we stand

The smoke
And mirrorrs   the

                                              wink
                      the flaw —
The

                                    Head
Where others,   not
Protected

                    wanted to get out
        some

                    would

blur the

                    grieved
               thought
How   some
               should come to

    Death —

         comprehend

                    ?
               trust the
                              head?
          impeach

    And   brake

Him

D
own

So foreign   —

He

could not bear   ,
wished they'd

stayed away

            acknowledge
      their unthinking

                  picture —
It's   impossibility

      sweet

      talk, like
      the
Raised
      easy

         Balloon

awful

to

          live to know

such a day

.

.

silenced,

I'm different

My
face

will
turn   to
one long

look of

hungry

Hope

the Infinite

shall

trust

me

— I've stopped being Their's —

Called to
Existence

half   conscious   —
But
With Will

such and such

in the Sepulchre —

on such a
date —

You try to

tell

the Company

That dont remember

It was not

It was
their

was not   Flesh

just

Figures

       fitted to a frame
       could not breathe

                     ticked
And

        the Beating

                 — Stopless —
Without a Chance

     I could see

      fear

         when his life was out —

uncertain

if it was there —

the Owner

pushed   and waited —

Conviction

too

easy

did not know I saw —

He

       looked   frightened

Like one in danger

The   Bandaged

    feel   Fright
And

    freezing   —

          escape

    a Bomb

Long Dungeoned

    the news of

their

bright

Lives

Spare

d

keep

our

Heart

almost

Content

he
practised

Recording

soft Refrains

of Adamant

to
numb

our
Children to

dumb the
Revelations

He
— in silence —
hid

to make

Death's   stare —

Look
          not
                    too

                    strong   —

But   he

                    failed!

          for what wrong
          did

their

Head
s fall

they held —

they bore

He
Spoke of
That   journey —

Heaven —

wealth   —
happy — happy   —

just abroad

boldly
tell Him   No —
No —
interdict —

fictitious

the
everlasting
perfect
Delight

Blesseder
then
To

save
another

a   feeling

Yesterday

Of Ground

letting go

—

1862.27 (373–375)

This World

baffles —

Men
of

Faith slip — and
see
Evidence —

in
lies —

their

Reward for   this —

Empire

the old — road —
unfrequented —

she passed —

swift —

Look!
turn   back

Herself —   fled!

Another bed
     make

     out of sight —
For
          her Head!

          in
     which   chamber is

                    the
     Maelstrom

               ?

who heard
        the Birds

    knew

No one could
                    perfect
            that

                                Eden —

                    surrender
        the

        legend
    and the
            telling

When the last
                    silence
        strikes

Sphere of

too common

perishing —

dream

the letters I can write

were

dance

Or

                    —like Birds —

                    sound,

    mention
                    me

    coming Home

        to stay

    I

            have a way —

a Pile of Mountains —

crawl between

chase

Then
Stop —

It don't sound so terrible   as it did —
I

Shift
            To

new Things —

It's shrewd

        the

Next — One —
Could

                mend my old One —

And   mine —
      the joy of feeling

high —

when I die

      — how rich I go —
    impeach
And banish me —

the fair Ideal,

we discover

a lie —

We adored

Him —

Obedient to

command

It would never be

that   sort

now

As

all the World

suddenly   shrank

back

They   remember
the

People

of Death —

how to forget

they

died

In
Sacrifice

But

to

an

invention

Of

cool

Disposers —

we

occupy

another

One

not

meant

For

us

again —

The   last

            hand
                        was my
                                                Raise

He

                took   —
                                paid
            The   price,

                        handed me
            A single

                        broke forth
            And
                                        ran

he thought
men

did not Care

here
They'd modify

Judgment

— Surrender   — Cancel

And leave   alone —

I think

It suits

That men

in the Desert

The Gnash of   thrive   on

play,

And

Dare

the Fire's
vivid

conditions —

it's

soundless

Refining

Blaze

To hear   sing
      a common

      Crowd

"No Sir!   "
           is
    Anguish

But

       we could die —
The best

  reason

To put this   down
And walk   away

his   Confederates

                       sowed
Clusters

every drop

    put away   life

     low as mine
might have been

  sowed
              pain,
Or
Or

     the least
  just
       delighted it

A
  "Hide and Seek"—
Or
Or   chase   —

The Surgeon will not
          will have   to
          will

          will

               may

     Over and over

the

Haunted

Brain

meeting

it

self   —

in
Horror   —

borrows a Revolver

More

Old fashioned

Tradition

Society —

Unmoved —   notes

an ample nation

in

pain —

And   turned

Mine —   the   Election!
Mine
Mine

Mine
Mine

Mine —   A   steal!

She   at

          Arms,
As if for   sport —

Her   Eyes

     sparkling

Devising   a
     force
               so deep

          it
Could not   be proved

     our idea

To Him
     'tis

       solemn!

       the   Press
   Imagery

      Parades —

Flags,   a brave sight —

      triumphant —

             He went

Lit with

A Power

     just adequate

    — an Ampler Zero —

Citizen

Who
Ignores the   News

The   ends

        of

                        lives

                put away —

By

        His

        power

Riches —

Dominions —

the Commonest

Wealth

Without a stint —

each Day,

solaces

I prove

It's

simple

Death is   Common

      privilege

              is large

       a   Thing
So
Naked

Which

                Forces

That
    far

          trouble
             back—

      altered,

I

                nestled Close

To Cushions

'twas
Peace —

Give little
Lives

   they'll

  make no

          Speech

       a thing

      to atoms blown —

   another
      Day

        my face

      begun to laugh —

And
My Brain keeps giggling —

   Something's odd —

Could it be Madness

Grave
Grave

help

Grave
Grave

Grave

You've seen

it   before

the Agony

Toyed coolly with

you

Until you felt your

Sense   numb —

your

                    Doubt

            the utterest —

I gave Myself to

The solemn

Vision

in the

subtle   lie —

Some

predicted

them

do   us

wrong

We

witness

A Moment

fit our Vision to the Dark

And meet the

        larger — Darkness

The Bravest
            hit
Directly

                know 'tis
   Glory —

   Glory

             and

      Might
Assert themselves —

The Lady

peers beyond her mesh —

contented —

Think of it Lover!
           face to face
                    we'll say

How Midnight felt
How all the Clocks stopped   the World
                              'Twas so cold

We look back
At those Old Times

to look at

Paradise

my sentence

extremest

shame —

"God have mercy" on the Soul

at the last,

Salute, and pass,
there, the Matter Ends —

in the Trees

find

A long — long Yellow

Our

Hurrying Home
To
All

Of

them

I promised ne'er to
break My word

No fear

It is dead —
Out of Sight —
Which is wiser —
You, or the

low Ground?

in this World

this   is said to be

rare —
to

choose

some one else
And leave
Himself

in the Dark —

Home
like Paradise

never comes

they say

Myself would run

to
It's

secure — inviting —

shelter

I had been

trembling

hungry,

could not hope

did not know

felt ill — and odd —
                                    Bush

                            found
                    a way
Of
        entering

My   Life

I leaned upon the Awe —

                    an Ocean
        broke against my ear —

                fear
                        compassed

                me

You'll find — it
easier to
recollect

their
names

when this

tawdry

Love of
Viole

n
c
e

be

held

for

Nought

And   a living child —

                more
Than
           a

        Gnat

They shut   up

For Treason

Him

That

         was not

unconscious

a Man

                they
        know

could be heard

Oh, Reward

                for Truth

Dreams — are   better

       at

            confronting

        the

         Axis

      — spin

      paints

It's   precise
      Brand

On

The   whole

          feared

                    Destiny

                         — Home —

     Borne on

                    fit

                    gain

we

     stand up   —

        some sovreign

few
Smile — and alter — and prattle —

Our journey
     almost
To that
     Term

    took sudden awe —

Forest of the Dead —

Retreat — was out

    because
    it would be

power dropped —

I sang firm

I

               must pass

Through

      the Grave —

       Worlds

   we

          knew not   till then

They

    did not dare
For fear

              of

The

    Prison

        to look
For the
    deal   stated as Our

Posture
That
                    — Not so real
        Liberty —

        something passiver —

        Liberty
                like a Dream
            for any

1862.57 (457–461)

Sometimes

they do not die —

who have

bared
a Bone —

Steel's
grimace in the Flesh —
How

— not polite —

to

require

149

reasons

Therefore —

Transport
    such
        Tent by Tent
            Flags

    Cover
Not
                     Us —

    notice Us — no more —
                turn away
        o'er and o'er

The General

— dazzling pace —

makes no show for

An independent   —

Was ever   like

   the

other   s
the Twitter
opposite

the Whole —

wished a way
to
magnify
the

Blood
opon
the Road —

far

away —

Possibility —

Superior —

for an everlasting

Occupation —

A Solemn thing
To
            hang
The Maker   —
        the
            Being

You thought was finished —

But
Your   Harvest
        — Every sun
    —   some lives.

Gulf
          of solid Blood -
          the

          appointed Creature

     bows   and

     fetches

And
     could be

               like

The Minor One   that

               cared to please

          the mighty

none could see

I was

    stationed
                    —

  just
      think
That   was all —

  never spoke — unless addressed —

The Racket shamed me   —

     had not been
     one I knew

       — I

                cannot see -

  further

    pretending

To

                                    toil
Against   Man
                   — I

Relate
                  to
           them —

He

      stuns you by Degrees —

     the   Blow
                      further
Then nearer — Then

       your naked soul —

              in their Paws —

Adamant

put
agonizing terms

down

I could not stop

My labor

We passed the
Recess -

He passed Us
The   Chill
    on

the Ground —

Since then — 'tis

Eternity -

He   like those Who've nought to lose
Bestowed   to

Us

Men,

His Comrades

left alive
to die

to justify

This   honorless
futile Diadem —

the
General

Rendered
"Sweet"
Liberty

won   by

possession —
in the land —

Could I

Not opon   knee   thank

And

Praise

the

Benefactor
Making

Blank
A   Way

To   advance

ends
    disclosed —

it came
by degrees -

reprieves

long enough for

rallying
—

a

kiss
with

Mother
Or Father —

on the Lawn
Indicative that

Darkness   is about to pass

I deemed

     therefore

That I   adjust

My Faith
  when
My Faith

               steps

          abroad
To do His   Will

How dare I

                    fail

The

               Men —

We want
Honors —

Flags —

a friend's Hand —

the Ministry

       —

To offer brave
   Lives

            Divine

            Benediction

Not a
            cool
Hope
Not

                    lying   —
    Yet   Nature

                        was still —

                    forget
                        that
                        —

    Memory

                did'nt come

                                Declare —
        Were you   there?

His business
has been

To

fling Sand,

                    "Get out of the Way, I say"
Who'd
Would you
            be the fool to stay?

The Day
                    of Gold
            of Purple
            old

            as the World
And yet

Too near

        Candle
        Flickering

            in the Cold
                    Trudging
            World —

The Cruel — smiling —   World —
            it's

                    forgotten —
The

                Hands
Lifted

        supplicate

One
        be finished

The
        Danger
Is

                    — opon the Soul

To go without
        challenging Despair.

People and events referenced in the poems, and occasional speakers of the poems, include those piloting aircraft on 9/11; U.S. President George W. Bush; Osama bin Laden; U.S. Vice President Dick Cheney; U.S. Defense Secretary Donald Rumsfeld; the pro-war Republican Congress (the elephant is the symbol of the Republican Party in the U.S.); soldiers, terrorists, occupiers, insurgents, and combatants on both sides of both the wars in Afghanistan and Iraq; Afghani and Iraqi civilians; *Wall Street Journal* reporter Daniel Pearl; British Prime Minister Tony Blair; prisoners at Abu Ghraib and Guantanamo Bay facilities and their guards; those injured by improvised explosive devices, gunfire, bombs, and other means; Pfc. Lynndie England; Spc. Charles Graner; families of those killed on 9/11; families of U.S. soldiers killed in Iraq and Afghanistan; war resisters both inside and outside the military; Muslim and Christian religious leaders; U.S. Secretary of State Condoleeza Rice; the phenomenon of displaying yellow ribbons to indicate one "has not forgotten" soldiers fighting the war; former Ambassador Joseph C. Wilson, IV; the "Bush Doctrine"; Gen. Peter Pace; and Gen. David Petraeus.

AUTHOR

Janet Holmes is author of *F2F, Humanophone, The Green Tuxedo,* and *The Physicist at the Mall.* She is editor of Ahsahta Press and a professor in the MFA program for creative writers at Boise State University. She lives in Idaho with her husband, the novelist and poet Alvin Greenberg.

CPSIA information can be obtained
at www.ICGtesting.com
Printed in the USA
FSOW01n0356270115
4742FS

9 781848 610354